anaging

aud and Corruption Risk

cal Government

i

Managing Fraud and Corruption Risk in Local Government

How to make your Council Fraud Resistant

David Grugeon
CPA (CPA Australia),
FCA (England and Wales)

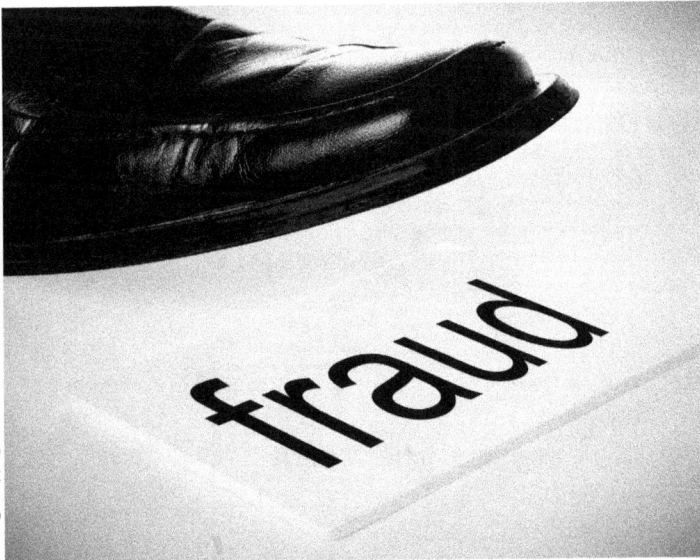

First published 2014 by Grubooks
PO Box 2189 Chermside Centre Queensland 4032 Australia
© Grugeon Consulting 2016
The moral rights of the author have been asserted
National Library of Australia Cataloguing-in-Publication data:

Creator	Grugeon, David, 1943- author.
Title:	Managing fraud and corruption risk in local government : how to make your council fraud resistant / David Grugeon.
ISBN:	9781925319033 (paperback)
	9781925319026 (ebook : pdf)
	9781925319040 (ebook : epub)
Notes	Includes bibliographical references.
Subjects:	Fraud--Government policy--Australia.
	Local government--Australia.
	Fraud--Australia--Prevention.
	Political corruption--Australia--Prevention.
Dewey Number	364.1630994

Disclaimer

The material in this publication is of the nature of general comment only and is not intended to be advice for a specific local government or other organisation. Readers should not act on information given in this publication without considering (and, if appropriate, taking) professional advice on their own particular circumstances. The publisher and author expressly disclaim any liability to any person or organisation because of any action taken or not taken in reliance, in whole or in part, on the content of this publication.

Contact the Author
David Grugeon
PO Box 2189 Chermside Centre Qld 4032
Phone 0429 029 836
Email: david@grugeon.com.au
Web: www.grugeon.com.au

To Elizabeth, whose persistence and support made this book happen

Table of Contents

Introduction

Why is a book about fraud and corruption in local government important at the present time?

Local governments are experiencing a time of increased pressure to do more with less, reduced central government funding, and great difficulties obtaining suitable and competent staff. This puts considerable pressure on senior management who are working harder than ever trying to maintain services for their communities.

In 2015, fraud and corruption resulted in significant cost to local governments. Councils rarely recover losses from fraud and corruption.

A recent study of fraud and corruption prevention methods in local government (1) carried out by the Queensland Audit Office reported that the cost of recovering money lost through fraud and corruption typically resulted in expenditure of three times the amount recovered.

The same study found that few local governments had adequate policies and provisions in place to deter or prevent fraud and corruption.

Governance of councils determines how they go about achieving their objectives and impacts on whether or not they achieve those objectives. The management of risk, and particularly the risks of fraud and corruption, is one of the key pillars of governance.

If the prevention of fraud and corruption is not a primary focus of management, opportunities will exist for potential fraudsters to exploit. Traditionally fraud resistance has been just an afterthought in putting together the code of conduct and the procurement policy, rather than being a core element of the way a council operates in all areas of its business. This is similar to the changes seen in recent years to the approach to workplace health and safety.

This book will assist local government in putting in place a suitable environment and adequate measures for the reduction of fraud and corruption, thereby saving themselves significant amounts of inappropriate expenditure and losses while improving their reputation and the integrity of their procedures and operations.

The book provides information to assist councils in changing their focus from a passive and reactive approach to fraud and corruption to an active and proactive state of being highly resistant to fraud.

This book will be particularly relevant to CEOs; Mayors; Chairmen, and members, of Audit Committees; and Administration/Corporate Services Managers, as they work to make their councils fraud resistant.

Reducing the occurrence of fraud in local government will make more money and resources available for the priorities of the council, and will improve the status of local government and the well-being of their communities.

Whilst we have written this book against the background of the legislation in Queensland, Australia, the principles and methods suggested are also applicable in other States and Territories and elsewhere in the world. Unfortunately, fraud and corruption in local government is not just a local problem but also a global one.

I hope you find this book helpful in developing fraud resistance in your organisation. If you do please let me know and tell your colleagues. If you have any issues or suggestions for improvement, or if you want any further information or assistance, please tell me. Contact details are on the page iv.

David Grugeon

1   Definitions of Fraud and Corruption

Since there are many different definitions of Fraud and Corruption in different legislation and other sources, we will use a simplified definition in this book. You should refer to the full definitions in the legislation and standards (reproduced below) for accuracy in relation to the particular legislation.

For the purposes of this book, we define

Fraud and corruption

- **Fraud** is obtaining a personal advantage through deception.
- **Corruption** is using a position of power or trust to obtain a personal advantage.
- **Personal advantage** includes advantage for family, friends, associates, or an entity connected to a person. It also includes an unwarranted disadvantage to another person.
- A **position of trust** includes any public office, employment, appointment, or contract.
- Theft from an employer is taken to be **fraud**.
- **Corrupt behaviour** may be by an entity other than a person.
- **Corrupt behaviour** includes enabling another to engage in corrupt behaviour.
- **Governance** comprises the processes (including policies, procedures, and actions) of management (elected council and executive management) by which an organisation (the council) achieves its objectives.
- We also use the term **council worker** to refer to any of:
  - The Mayor
  - Councillors
  - Chief Executive Officer

- ○ Directors/Managers
- ○ Other Council Employees whether part- or full-time, permanent or temporary
- ○ Person working under a contract for services or their employees (e.g. Consultants)
- ○ Contract employees, and
- ○ Volunteers

Official definitions are:

Fraud	Dishonest activity causing actual or potential financial loss to any person or entity including theft of moneys or other property by employees or persons external to the entity and where deception is used at that time, immediately before or immediately following the activity. This also includes the deliberate falsification, concealment, destruction or use of falsified documentation used or intended for use for a normal business purpose or the improper use of information or position for personal financial benefit The theft of property belonging to an entity by a person or persons internal to the entity but where deception is not used is also considered 'fraud' for the purposes of the Standards.	Australian Standard AS 8001-2008 (2)
Corruption	Corrupt conduct is: conduct of a person, regardless of whether the person holds or held an appointment, that—	Crime and Corruption Act 2001 (Qld) s.15 (3)

	<ul><li>adversely affects, or could adversely affect, directly or indirectly, the performance of functions or the exercise of powers of—<ul><li>a unit of public administration (UPA)</li></ul> or <ul><li>an individual person holding an appointment in a UPA</li></ul></li><li>results, or could result, directly or indirectly, in the performance of functions or the exercise of powers mentioned above in a way that—<ul><li>is not honest or is not impartial</li><li>involves a breach of the trust placed in a person holding an appointment, either knowingly or recklessly</li><li>involves a misuse of information or material acquired in or in connection with the</li></ul></li></ul>	

	performance of functions or the exercise of powers of a person holding an appointment • is engaged in for the purpose of providing a benefit to the person or another person or causing a detriment to another person • would, if proved, be— - a criminal offence or - a disciplinary breach providing reasonable grounds for terminating the person's services, if the person is or were a holder of an appointment.	
Public Interest Disclosure	A Public Interest Disclosure is defined in Part 2 of the Act.	Public Interest Disclosure Act 2010 (4)
Governance	Broadly speaking, 'corporate governance' refers to the processes by which organisations are directed, controlled and held to account. It encompasses authority, accountability, stewardship,	Australian National Audit Office – Public Sector Governance Volume 1 (5)

leadership, direction and control exercised in the organisation.

Public sector governance has a very broad coverage, including how an organisation is managed, its corporate and other structures, its culture, its policies and strategies and the way it deals with its various stakeholders. The concept encompasses the manner in which public sector organisations acquit their responsibilities of stewardship by being open, accountable and prudent in decision making, in providing policy advice, and in managing and delivering programs.

Objectives of public sector governance

Public sector governance aims to ensure that an organisation achieves its overall outcomes in such a way as to enhance confidence in the organisation, its decisions and its actions. Good governance therefore means that the organisation's leadership, its staff, the Government, the Parliament and the population can rely on the organisation to do its work well and with full probity and accountability.

Good governance generally focuses on two main requirements of organisations:

- **performance,** whereby the organisation uses its

| | governance arrangements to contribute to its overall performance and the delivery of its goods, services or programs; and

• **conformance,** whereby the organisation uses its governance arrangements to ensure it meets the requirements of the law, regulations, published standards and community expectations of probity, accountability and openness.
Risk management should underpin the organisation's approaches to achieving both performance and conformance objectives. An integrated risk management system develops the control environment, which provides reasonable assurance that the organisation will achieve its objectives with an acceptable degree of residual risk. | |

2 Fraud and corruption risk in local government

2.1 What is the risk?

The nature of fraud and corruption is that they are disguised and hidden activities. For this reason, and because entities which have suffered fraud and corruption are frequently reluctant to make this public, the available statistics on levels of fraud and corruption probably only reflects a proportion of the total amount which actually takes place.

A recent study by Chartered Accountants Australia and New Zealand (6) says that, in Australia and New Zealand, looking only at instances reported which were in excess of one million dollars, there was an 82% increase in the level of fraud, bribery, and corruption for all entities and there was a 300 per cent increase in losses between 1997 and 2012.

The QAO report (1) said that Queensland councils detected 324 cases of alleged and confirmed fraud between 1 July 2009 and November 2014 involving $8.6 million. There were 18 cases of fraud greater than $10,000.

Bearing in mind that there were undoubtedly some undetected cases, this is a considerable cost to local governments, substantially reducing the amount they could spend on projects benefitting their communities and fulfilling their objectives.

Apart from the financial cost, fraud and corruption also have a serious impact on the reputation and integrity of the local government. The shadow of identified corruption is not limited to the corrupt individual alone, but impacts on the reputation of the whole Council.

2.2 How well does local government handle this risk?

The QAO report (1) reached the conclusion that "Most councils are not effective in managing their fraud risks – fraud and corruption is happening in councils, but few understand sufficiently how widespread is, or what it costs them."

It appears that the councils simply do not have the appropriate frameworks in place at all levels and in all areas to reduce the likelihood of fraud and corruption, to detect it if it does happen, or to take appropriate action if it is detected.

2.3 Why is local government vulnerable?

Local government is particularly vulnerable to fraud and corruption for a number of reasons:

- They deal with large amounts of money
- There is a frequent turnover of staff
- Senior staff are supervising a wide range of activities
- Pressure to "get the job done" may mean that controls are overridden and supervision may be inadequate.
- In smaller councils particularly, funding may be insufficient to allow separation of duties to be an adequate control.

Local government councillors are not subject to integrity checks and the motivation for standing for election as a Councillor may be to achieve some personal gain or benefit. Although the legislation is quite clear, some councillors may be subject to considerable temptation or pressure to make decisions that are not necessarily in the public interest.

Ratepayers, council customers, and members of the community may put employees under pressure to make decisions favouring them.

Unless there is a strong ethical environment in the council, employees and councillors may not realise that they have a duty, in making decisions, to make those decisions purely in the public interest. Even if they do understand this responsibility, they may perceive it as secondary to keeping the community members happy.

2.4 What can councils do?

A council can choose to be fraud-resistant. If it does not become fraud resistance, or adopts a piecemeal approach to managing the fraud risk, it will be vulnerable to fraud.

A picture of a fraud-resistant Council would include the following features:

- The elected body has defined what they consider to be a fraud and corruption and their level of tolerance for fraud. This would normally be a zero tolerance.
- The CEO has given a clear direction in writing to all members of staff and contractors to make it clear that the council will not allow any corrupt or fraudulent practice.
- A comprehensive fraud and corruption control plan has been prepared, based on a rigorous analysis of the fraud risks. This is regularly reviewed, is available to all staff, and is the basis for continuing action to manage the risks.
- The risks of fraud in all Council sections are effectively analysed, at least every two years, and this analysis is the basis for preventative controls and action.
- The need to prevent and avoid fraud and corruption, is addressed, significantly, in staff induction, regular staff meetings, and specific regular training.
- Council policies, and in particular the procurement and employee engagement policies, and the codes of conduct for employees, consultants and contractors, include appropriate anti-fraud measures.
- The Council takes regular action to detect possible or likely fraud. This action may, for example, include data analytics.
- A person or persons to whom suspected fraud can be reported, has been nominated and those persons have a clear understanding what action to take when they receive such reports.

- All councillors, employees, contractors, and consultants, are aware of who to report to and how. The information is also prominently displayed on the website and on posters in public areas of the council buildings.
- A specific policy on the prevention of fraud and on the actions that will be taken if fraud or corruption are detected, has been adopted and is regularly reviewed.

The main feature of a fraud-resistant Council is that there is a broad understanding and acceptance at all levels that fraud is unacceptable and harmful to the interests of the community, the council, and all the people who work there.

This ethical standing cannot be achieved instantly, neither is it the product of specific action, but rather the result of clear leadership and a sustained commitment to resist fraud.

Fraud prevention is closely linked to risk management. If the council has a thorough risk management process, it will have identified fraud and corruption as risks. Treatment of those risks will necessarily involve all or most of the steps set out in this book.

Councils, traditionally, have not regarded fraud and corruption as separate risks needing their own approach to treatment, but have rather looked at the separate areas of the business where fraud and corruption could take place. The use of a comprehensive fraud and corruption control strategy is more likely to result in effective minimisation of fraud and corruption incidents in the council.

An outline of an appropriate and effective method for assessing and analysing fraud and corruption risks is included at section 7.

3   Some examples of fraud and corruption

The following examples indicate the broad range of activities that could be considered fraudulent or corrupt behaviour. The list is not intended to be exhaustive.

A councillor's wife owns some land through a nominee company and the councillor does not disclose this in the register of interests. The Councillor urges the CEO and the other councillors to support a planning application in respect of that land.

An employee of the council takes her work laptop computer home saying that she needs to do some Council work on it (which is true). She then uses the computer to prepare accounts for her personally owned business.

The Works Manager overestimates the quantity of material for a job. He then arranges for the excess to be delivered to his home.

The debtors clerk finds that a customer has overpaid. She raises a refund of the overpaid amount payable to her partner's bank account.

The creditors clerk enters an invoice twice. Both are paid. He then arranges to split the difference with the supplier.

The Corporate Services Manager (CSM) is arranging for expressions of interest for a new computer system. One supplier is a subsidiary of an Italian company. This supplier arranges for the CSM to spend two weeks in Italy, all expenses paid, to see the proposed system in operation.

The local laws officer has permission to take a Council vehicle home in case he is called out to an emergency. The vehicle is to be used for Council purposes only. On his way home, he picks up his children from school.

The Administration Manager receives a Christmas gift of a bottle of premium whisky from the manager of a stationery supplier.

The HR manager appoints her daughter as an assistant. Since the HR manager knows her daughter's abilities, she does not advertise the position or go through formal selection procedures.

An employee is in control of the council grants to sporting bodies. The chairman of the local netball club cuts in front of him on his way to work. Later that day, he assesses the grant applications, and recommends that the netball club application be turned down. There is no evidence that the netball club is less deserving than the hockey club, which is awarded $100,000.

The IT coordinator is dismissed. Before he left, he set a program to delete all the wage records a week after his termination was recorded on the system

4 Setting the tone

The tone of the local government is set primarily by those at the top. That is the Mayor, Councillors, and CEO.

The elected Mayor and Councillors should make a clear statement that fraud and corruption by any person in relation to the council will not be tolerated. This covers, not only the councillors and employees, but also contractors working for the council, and other people the council may deal with commercially. It is also important that the council itself is not involved in corruption, for example, by paying bribes or other similar incentives.

The CEO needs to make the council's position on fraud and corruption clear by writing a letter to all employees and contractors

- Making clear the zero tolerance of fraud and corruption.
- Including definitions of fraud and corruption.
- Giving clear guidance on what action should be taken if there is a suspicion that fraud or corruption may have occurred or be likely to occur.
- Stating the consequences for any council employee, contractor, or other person who is found to be involved.

Given the significant decisions made on behalf of councils by consultants and contractors, it is important that the fraud and prevention tone is extended to them. This cannot be achieved purely by including terms in the contract, but must include an induction process for consultants and contract staff.

The fraud and corruption resistant stance will be a key element in regular staff meetings. This ensures that managers and staff at all levels adopt the required ethical attitude and vigilance.

To help ensure that businesses dealing with the council adopt the required tone, the council would be well advised to make it a condition of each the tender or request for offers of a significant value that the business they are dealing with has a sound anti-corruption policy itself. For smaller contracts where there is no obvious risk, it may be sufficient to get the contractor/consultant to sign an undertaking to comply with the council's fraud and corruption policies and procedures.

The Council could also verify, for significant contracts, that the directors or owners of the business have not been convicted of fraud or corruption, or disqualified as a director. This can be done by carrying out criminal history checks and examining the register on the ASIC website.

Apart from adopting a formal framework for fraud, the tone must be set by example and action. The CEO and management team must demonstrate by their actions that they do not support or condone fraud in any way.

If the CEO appoints his wife as a manager, particularly without going through a formal and open merit selection procedure, then this gives a signal to employees that nepotism, and by implication other types of fraud, are acceptable.

If the CEO only uses a Council car strictly for Council business purposes this is an indication to others that this is the high standard expected.

The appropriate tone must be actively maintained by the management team and opportunities must be sought to reinforce the messages.

5   Risk reduction framework

The Council must introduce a comprehensive framework to reduce the risk of fraud or corruption occurring. This framework includes:

- A clear statement by the CEO provided to all staff, consultants, and those with whom the council proposes to do business setting out the position of the council.
- A policy on the prevention of fraud and corruption risk, adopted by the council (elected body).
- Proactive fraud risk assessment processes.
- Specific controls in policies and procedures designed to minimise fraud risk.
- Training of employees, contract staff, and consultants, on fraud and corruption minimisation.
- Effective reporting and recording both internally and externally.

One factor which is found in some entities with effective fraud control is the appointment of an Integrity Officer (IO). This person is responsible, under the CEO, for:

- developing, implementing, and maintaining the policy,
- conducting the training,
- facilitating the risk assessment by managers and others,
- receiving all reports of suspected or identified fraud and corruption,
- notifying authorities as appropriate,
- ensuring the appropriate records are kept,
- advising the CEO on action to be taken, and
- advising employees and others who may have potential ethical issues such as conflict of interest.

The IO may also conduct analysis of fraud risk and whether the controls continue to be effective, or this may be included in the work of the Internal Auditor or another person.

The IO need not be a full time employee but could be part time, a consultant or the duties could be added to an existing position if a suitably experienced person is available and has time to spare.

Under legislation, certain reporting and recording is required to be done by the CEO, but improvements in the quality and efficiency can be achieved by delegating these functions to a specialist. The legislation in different jurisdictions may vary.

Note: In this book it is assumed that an Integrity Officer is appointed. If there is no IO, then the duties will need to be allocated to someone else.

The framework must be well documented. A framework that is well worked out and covers all the points but sits in the CEO's head, will fall over as soon as the CEO gets interested in a new idea. A framework that is written down and has specific action points assigned to individuals, with target dates, will be effective.

As with any change, the change management project will only succeed if it is well planned, properly financed, and carried out with commitment.

Given the need to provide regular feedback to achieve goals, the planning should be detailed. To gain the commitment of all stakeholders it needs to be structured so that positive events – milestones achieved, targets met, changes made – will occur frequently. This planning needs to involve all levels of staff so there is ownership, the targets are achievable, and the achievements can be anticipated.

6   Council/CEO statement

A draft statement is at Appendix 8.

The CEO Statement, which reflects the views of the elected body, is an essential element of establishing an anti-fraud tone in a Council. The statement needs to be brief but cover the essentials:

- What are fraud and corruption.
- Fraud and corruption will not be tolerated in the council environment.
- In broad terms, the consequences for an individual or business engaging in fraud or corrupt conduct.
- The need to report all identified or suspected fraud or corrupt conduct immediately.
- To whom it should be reported.

The statement should be in clear and simple language. It may cross reference other sources for further information, but it is more important to get the message across than to ensure complete accuracy by using legal definitions.

This statement should be distributed to all staff (In their initial information package or during their initial training), to all contractors and consultants as or before they arrive to commence work, and to all people doing business with the council. Existing businesses will need to have a special mailing, perhaps with a covering letter explaining the context. For future business arrangements, a copy should be included with the formal request for a quotation, or with the tender documents.

The statement should also be placed prominently on the council's website. This gives a clear message to those having dealings with the council that they should not ask for favours, nor attempt to receive them. It will also go some way to reinforcing the reputation of the council as a "clean" council.

7 Risk Assessment

The assessment of the risk from Fraud and Corruption is a bit different from the normal assessment of operational risks because it involves thought processes that may not be familiar to managers. The process needs to be facilitated by an experienced practitioner. The council may consider engaging a consultant to facilitate this process.

The risk assessment team should be led by someone familiar with fraud and corruption – perhaps the integrity officer, if one has been appointed. The other members should be the senior management team of the council with perhaps some second-tier managers as well. Since fraud may involve considerations of procurement, assets, cash, and financial risk it is probably appropriate for the finance manager or accountant to be involved.

The team should consider each area of the operations of the council and, thinking like a fraudster, consider how fraud might be carried out in that area.

In looking at each area the team should look for:

- Decision making which could be impartial or inappropriate
- Theft or misuse of Council property whether fixed assets or supplies
- Misappropriated money
- Personal advantage including advantage to relatives or friends
- Non merit-based engagements, or promotions

The team needs to consider

- Factors creating temptation (e.g. easy access to material stocks)
- Relationships or potential relationships – particularly between those making decisions and the persons the decisions are made about (e.g. how well does the gardener know the garden centre owner).
- The degree of actual supervision in place

- The extent to which duties can realistically be divided.

The team then assesses the impact of the potential fraud in terms of consequence and likelihood, and considers any existing or possible controls.

Consequence has to be based on a compound scale considering

- Possible financial loss
- Impact on operations
- Physical or mental health risks to any person
- Political impacts
- Reputational damage to the council, Council management, or to the local government system as a whole.

Generally, there will be a quantified scale for each of these, with the highest level of impact determining the consequence rating.

The level of likelihood and the consequence rating give a total risk rating.

The results of this process are recorded in a risk register and form the basis for prioritising potential improvements to policies, procedures and controls. Existing risk treatment is recorded and new or additional measures may be implemented as indicated.

8   Fraud and corruption risk policy

This policy is the basis for all the council's measures to combat fraud and corruption. It formalises the council approach, sets out the actions that will be taken, and the procedures required under the framework.

It is a formal document which will relate the practical definitions and approach to fraud and corruption, to the technical definitions in the legislation and standard.

The policy will have the following elements:

- Authority, scope and review requirements
- Overview and purpose
- Policy in relation to:
    - Actions to minimise the risk of fraud and corruption
    - Actions to identify fraud and corruption
    - Processes for reporting suspected or actual fraud
    - Actions to deal with fraud and corruption when suspected or identified
- Procedures required to comply with the policy.

The policy is likely to include the basis for appointment and role of the Integrity Officer.

The policy should address the issues taking into account how any measures will impact on the different stakeholders: Mayor, Councillors, CEO, Management, Employees and Volunteers, Businesses the council deals with, and the local community.

A sample policy is included at Appendix 6.

9 Other policies

All policies should be reviewed to ensure they include appropriate provisions where required.

The Key policies and related documents that will need to include relevant matter will be:

- The Human Relations Management policies including those relating to appointment, termination of employment, induction, and training.
- The procurement policy and any other policies relating to tendering, procurement, or other dealings with businesses
- Codes of conduct for Councillors and employees
- Internal Audit Policy and Charter
- Audit Committee Policy and Charter
- Delegations by Council and by CEO
- Terms of employment and PDs

Content recommendations for some of these policies are included in the appropriate paragraphs in section 14.

10 Division of duties – practicalities

One common method of reducing the likelihood of fraud occurring is the division of duties. This means making sure that two different people are responsible for different parts of a transaction.

For example, the placing of orders may be the responsibility of a procurement officer, the processing of the resulting invoice may be the responsibility of the creditors clerk, and the payment of the invoice may be made by the cashier and authorised by the finance manager.

In this example there are, in theory, four people who know about the transaction and should have some understanding of it. Any one of those four may spot an irregularity which could lead to identifying the transaction as potentially fraudulent. To ensure the fraudulent activity is concealed, the perpetrator may have to get one or more of the four people to collude.

Division of duties therefore, is, on the face of it, a good method of reducing the risks. Collusion may be unlikely (depending on the relationship of the team members) so there is a deterrent in place. Rotating staff increases the likelihood of fraudulent activity being detected.

In practice we have to deal with the realities of human nature, which may render such division of duties less effective. Council employees may, for example, be presented with orders which are highly technical. The non-technical creditors clerk and cashier may not understand the technicalities and may not know enough to be able to identify inflated pricing or an order for quantities in excess of those required for the job.

The finance manager may be presented with a list of hundreds of payments to be made for approval. It is rare for a manager, in such a situation, to do more than glance at the list before approving it. The manager tends to trust the other officers to have carried out their duties and checked the detail.

Even if the procedure would be effective if implemented properly, in small councils there just may not be sufficient staff numbers to set up complete separation of duties. This will mean that, even though there may be appropriate procedures in place, they are carried out by the same people rather than separate people, with one person approving an order, entering the resultant invoice, and preparing the payment. This obviously requires the finance manager to be extra vigilant but in these small councils there may be considerable time pressure on the finance manager and this checking may well not receive the required attention.

In small councils, the small community which provides the source of the more junior levels of staff, results in Council staff members often being closely related or having strong personal relationships. This can result in an increased likelihood of collusion, or of excessive trust placed by one member of staff in another.

In designing internal controls of this nature, the risks of collusion in the particular environment need to be considered. A system of random audits by an external person may be more effective than the controls. Normally the detection of fraud is not considered part of the duties of the internal or external auditors. The internal auditor checks the controls that are in place to verify that they are functioning effectively; the external auditor checks with a view to ensuring the financial statements properly reflect the transactions of the council. While either of the above will have an interest in identifying fraud and will report it, if found, it is not a primary focus of their functions.

Internal auditors could be asked to carry out such checking as an additional task, which would normally involve an additional fee. Given the high risks and the potential for substantial loss, councils, particularly smaller ones, might consider this approach.

11 Small and remote Councils

Small and remote councils are in a very difficult position when it comes to fraud mitigation. They are subject to all the same requirements financially as larger councils. They are also subject to the same range of risks as larger councils, but the funds available to them are very much lower.

They also have significant difficulty attracting and retaining quality employees and, as mentioned above, the probability of close connections between employees is much higher than in a larger Council.

The risk of fraud is also increased when a Council is forced by its location to deal with a very limited range of suppliers.

However, because of the small budget of the council, the effect of any loss through fraud is proportionately much greater and the impact on the community and the council reputation from any corruption are also proportionately greater.

It is essential, therefore, that these smaller and remote councils make a particular effort to minimise fraud and corruption and its impact on the council.

Another risk, which is particularly likely in a small Council, is that the employees may be dominated by a manager or other executive to the point that they cannot, or do not, question attempts to override controls.

> *For example, the works manager may make arrangements to purchase items without obtaining the number of quotes required by the Procurement Policy. If the procurement clerk queries this, the manager may say that he knows this is the best deal, or that nobody else was willing to quote. He may make it clear that there will be adverse consequences, either in the clerk's employment or socially in the community, if the clerk continues "being difficult".*

Because of the small number of employees, there may be very little opportunity for job rotation. This makes it more likely that an employee can maintain particular fraudulent conduct over a long period.

Employees may be in the same position for many years and may carry out their job very effectively and with little supervision. This situation can give rise to risks of undetected fraud as the work may not be readily examined, or even understood, by other staff.

In view of the specialist knowledge required, it may be particularly appropriate for a small local government to utilise the services of its internal auditor or an external consultant, to monitor the management of fraud and corruption risk.

In setting up systems to manage fraud and corruption, risks a small council may need to obtain specialist skills and experience by engaging a consultant or utilising the services of its internal auditor.

12 Large Councils

In large councils, a different set of problems can arise. Firstly, there is an increased temptation for staff to become involved in fraud or corruption because the sums of money they are transacting are much greater. Secondly, there may be a very limited understanding by some employees of what other employees are doing. People tend to work in silos where sectional interests and loyalties conflict with Council-wide interests and loyalties. This can create a situation where Council departments "make their own rules" rather than follow Council-wide policies and procedures, thereby reducing the effectiveness of any counter-fraud measures imposed by the central administration.

There is, then, a need to have rigorous checking, by internal audit or otherwise, that the procedures put in place are followed, and not by-passed with the explanation that special processes are required for particular departments or sections.

The process of risk assessment in relation to Fraud and Corruption risk can be an effective means of bringing the managers of these silos in line with Council procedures and policies. This risk assessment, ideally, involves a facilitated process with a team of senior people from all areas of the council operations examining the work of each area and assessing the risks.

Larger councils may be able to provide full time, in house, resources to manage and implement their fraud and corruption risk management. It is essential to ensure that all aspects of council businesses and the businesses of controlled entities are considered.

13 Consultants and contract staff.

In some councils, consultants, directly or indirectly, play a large part in the management and administration of the council. Consultants such as consulting engineers may be responsible for the recommendation or approval of contracts for millions of dollars. It is essential that they apply the council policies scrupulously to these large tenders and contracts. It is therefore recommended that the same policies are applied to them as to employees of the council. Each individual who is involved in the processes should be required to attend induction training and to sign a copy of the council's policy or statement. Any individual who is unwilling to do so should be excluded from taking any part in assessing, recommending, or managing contracts. There may be a need to ensure that if any changes are made to the personnel engaged in a consulting contract the new people get appropriate induction training before any involvement.

Police checks may also be carried out on both the directors of the consulting firm and the individuals engaged in the work for the council. If there is any history of convictions for fraud or corruption or disqualification to act as a director of a company on the part of the directors, the council should consider terminating any engagements. If employees of the firm have been involved in fraud, the individual should be expressly excluded from any involvement with work for the council.

Many councils have people who ostensibly do work similar to employees but are hired from agencies or are engaged on a self-employed basis. These people should be subject to the same requirements as employees including police checks and induction training. Everyone who is part of the "Council Machine" must be on board, if the council, as an entity, is to achieve fraud resistance.

If employees of the council leave, and then work for the council, either as independent businesses or as contract staff, a red flag may be raised in considering fraud risks.

14 Fraud risk factors

Risk factors for fraud can arise from the setting, the procedures, or the people.

The setting is the local government which, as explained above, has particular vulnerabilities. These arise because of the type and volume of transactions, because of the diversity of operations, and because of the reasons some people become involved in local government.

The procedures may contain inadequate safeguards to prevent fraud and corruption occurring and may make it easy or hard for people to avoid them.

The setting and procedures factors will be examined particularly in the risk analysis process.

The remaining factor is the people. Fraud tends to occur when there is a combination of motivation or pressure on the individual, and opportunity, and an attitude or rationalisation that makes the person believe the fraud is acceptable.

The Fraud Triangle

This diagram shows how the three aspects are related to create the fraud risk.

The Motivation may just be greed but it is more often created from pressure on the individual arising from perceived difficulty keeping up with the peer group, difficulty meeting the person's own or spouse's financial needs, gambling or other addiction costs, or even an expansive lifestyle, not affordable from the person's income.

A good knowledge of the employees and the community may identify employees who are likely to be subject to this type of pressure. Other factors, such as delay in paying debts due to the council or frequent applications for wage advances, may be indicative of financial pressure.

The opportunity is discussed extensively elsewhere in this book. It will normally arise from inadequate controls or supervision.

The rationalization is a process in the person's mind where they can persuade themselves that it is acceptable to commit fraud. Some examples are:

- The Council is a big organisation so it will not hurt it to steal a little bit of money
- I should be paid more than I am (or I am working extra hours) so it is right for me to take the extra money
- The Council did not approve my planning application. That cost me lots, so the council owes me
- I have a duty to feed my children so the end justifies the means
- Other people are taking things so I can, too
- The Council has a duty to remove temptation. They have virtually asked me to take the money

If any of the three sides of the triangle can be removed the fraud risk is greatly reduced. Implementing effective controls will reduce the opportunity. A knowledge of employees' personal situations can make it easier to identify motivation risk. The rationalization aspect can only be approached through example, an appropriate organisational ethos, and training to reinforce this.

15 Red flags for fraud

Managers and employees responsible for Council resources should be aware of the red flags for fraud. These are warning signs that may indicate that fraud risk is higher. They are not evidence that fraud is actually occurring. The existence of one or two flags is not something to be overly concerned about. However, if multiple flags are present and accounting irregularities or weak controls are identified, then consideration needs to be given to further investigation.

Examples of red flags include the following:

Employee Red Flags

- Employee lifestyle changes: expensive cars, jewellery, homes, clothes
- Significant personal debt and credit problems
- Behavioural changes - These may be an indication of drugs, alcohol, gambling, or just fear of losing the job
- High employee turnover, especially in those areas which are more vulnerable to fraud
- Refusal to take vacation or sick leave

Management Red Flags

- Management frequently overrides internal controls
- Management decisions are dominated by an individual or small group
- Managers display significant disrespect for regulatory bodies
- Council-wide procedures not adopted by particular manager/department
- Policies and procedures are not documented or enforced
- Weak internal control environment
- Accounting personnel are lax or inexperienced in their duties
- Decentralisation/delegation without adequate monitoring
- Excessive number of year end transactions; unnecessarily convoluted transactions
- High employee turnover rate; low employee morale

- Refusal to use serial numbered documents (receipts, requisitions)
- Keeping corporate data on personal computer or under a password without valid reason
- Photocopied or missing documents
- Reluctance to provide information to management or auditors

16 Specific Areas
16.1 Procurement

Procurement is one of the major areas where fraud and corruption are likely to be encountered. Procurement deals with large sums of money (creating temptation and opportunity) and with a high volume of transactions (creating opportunities to hide fraudulent transactions).

Much procurement involves purchasing from local suppliers, and for political reasons this may be preferred. This increases the likelihood that a close relationship exists or is developed between the supplier and Council employees, increasing the risk of fraudulent activity.

Councils generally have a procurement policy and defined procedures for procurement. These need to be examined and tested against a range of possible fraudulent or corrupt scenarios.

Some of the ways fraud operates in relation to procurement are

- Orders recorded as placed for goods and services that are never actually supplied
- Orders placed at inflated prices
- Orders placed with friends or relations without ensuring best value for money and open competition
- Conspiracy between suppliers to artificially raise prices (including dummy tenders in a limited market)
- Misuse of preferred supplier lists to favour friends and relatives
- Over-ordering to create surplus supplies used by the perpetrator

There are many other scenarios.

The approach to dealing with procurement issues starts with a thorough analysis of the risks. Management will identify as many as possible of the ways fraud could happen. Then specific measures are introduced into the procurement policy and procedures to address these risks. Typical measures include: separation of the processes of ordering, receiving goods, and processing/paying invoices; managers checking lists of invoices relating to their departments; budgetary control; verification of cost overruns; application of data analytics; independent review of payments and paid invoices; and strict tender/offer procedures for larger contracts.

It is essential to ensure that, not only are appropriate policies and procedures in place, but that they are adhered to. This is an area that will need some independent checking by the Internal Auditor and by senior financial management. There are many reasons particular items may not fit the designed model – utility charges, for example. All these exceptions need to be explicitly dealt with in the policy and procedures, together with any measures necessary to compensate for the lack of standard controls.

Telephone accounts may not "fit in" with a policy which says 'every purchase must have a priced order signed by the manager responsible for the area.' Typically telephone bills cannot be quantified in advance and the telephone company has their own terms of business which would not be constrained by a priced order. The policy may therefore say 'Telephone bills must be paid on or before the due date. Any obvious errors will be raised with the supplier before that date. An analysis of the bill by department specifying the particular extensions and specifying all calls costing in excess of $20.00 must be prepared and supplied to the department managers within 2 weeks of the date of the bill. The department managers must investigate any apparent irregularities and report these if necessary. Having checked the analysis, the managers must sign and return the analysis to the Creditors Clerk by 4 weeks after the date of the bill. Any recovery of costs incurred by employees will be taken in accordance with the Use of Telephones policy'.

In addition, the council may graph telephone charges by month for each department to identify any rising trends for further investigation.

It is inevitable that after adoption of a new comprehensive procurement policy many items will be found to need exceptions.

These may be made by a supplement to the policy, but the need must be reviewed both by the relevant manager and a senior finance area representative, such as the Finance Manager, to ensure the exception is actually required, and that suitable alternative controls are in place.

16.2 Use of Council property

The principle to apply to use of Council property by employees, family, and friends, should be that employees should not obtain any advantage by reason of their employment.

If Council plant is made available for hire to the public, then it can be made available to employees on the same terms. Generally, the borrowing, or use, of Council equipment and plant for private purposes is not acceptable. Current trends in local government are to prohibit the use of Council equipment for private use completely, largely because of health and safety requirements, the risks of damage, and public perception.

There will be occasions when a vehicle has to be taken home because an employee is on-call or has to use it in the morning before the depot is open. This use should be the subject of a written permission setting out the terms of use which strictly exclude any private use. A log book should be maintained recording each journey, start and finish km, time, purpose of the journey, etc.

Council may engage senior employees on a contract that includes private vehicle use. The value of that benefit will be taken into account in assessing the level of remuneration to pay for the position. It should be understood that, because local governments pay a higher rate of FBT than the private sector, the cost of providing such a benefit is higher. It may be more effective to pay a higher salary and allow the employee to provide his own vehicle.

There is no objection to equipment such as Council laptops being taken home for use for Council work. However, there should be a specific written permission for the use by a particular employee. This should be signed by the employee to ensure that the employee understands that the equipment is to be used for Council purposes only, not for private use.

16.3 Private Works

As with plant hire, Council should not allow work to be carried out on the private property of employees, unless it runs a business of providing such services to the public — then the work should be on the same terms as it is provided to the public.

16.4 Asset disposal

Surplus materials and small plant should not be taken by employees. It is too difficult to distinguish between the accidental remaining material and deliberate over-ordering to create a surplus to be taken for private use. Practice with such surpluses should be to collect them in a secure location and periodically hold a public auction or tender process to dispose of them.

Any asset which has a value of over $1,000 is required to be disposed of by auction or tender (under the legislation in Queensland — the requirements may vary in other jurisdictions.). This does not just apply to non-current assets but to surplus materials, stores items, and any other Council property.

Procedures should be in place to examine each proposed disposal to ensure the surplus material has not been deliberately purchased to make it available for a cheap sale.

Small tools must be clearly marked as property of the council to discourage employees taking them and then reporting them as lost or damaged. A record of the tools issued to each employee might be an appropriate control to reduce the risk of employees obtaining tools and then retaining them for private use or private sale.

16.5 Cash handling

Many councils need to deal with large amounts of cash. Some, particularly small and remote councils, will act as de-facto banks for community members.

The risks involved are substantial, both because cash is normally unidentifiable, so if it is stolen there may be little chance of proving responsibility, and because the temptation to persons outside the council staff may generate other risks such as assault on staff.

Where possible, it is recommended that councils avoid handling large amounts of cash. This could be by making arrangements with a bank to open a community bank, or by encouraging community members to use on-line banking, rather than cash. A Council could make arrangements for community members to obtain fee-free basic bank accounts with on-line access.

If a Council has to handle cash, strict controls are needed to reduce temptation, safeguard staff, and ensure accountability, as well as to prevent loss of cash.

The controls must include full daily reconciliations, recording all transactions as they occur, and ensuring no one person handles a transaction without verification by another person. Physical security for cash and cash handling staff will be required while the cash is being handled, when it is left in the council offices outside office hours, and when it is being transported off-site

16.6 Risks particular to the IT area

Local government faces some risks in connection with IT that arise from the way IT operates in local government and particularly in smaller local governments. It also faces risks because of the nature of IT.

In smaller local governments, there is usually one employee who has a reasonable or good understanding of the IT setup. Typically, that employee will have a wide-ranging procurement function for IT hardware, software, services, and supplies. The employee also deploys the hardware and software, manages all maintenance issues, and makes recommendations on IT issues to senior management.

The total spend on IT can be significant and, often, no other employee has a good understanding of the interaction of the various supply functions.

The people, inside and outside the council, working in IT, particularly in IT for local government, form a close community. This can result in recommendations being made which favour associates of the recommender, and may not present the best long-term value.

One issue with IT is the heavy cost of changing systems. This tends to lock councils into a particular supplier, particularly for financial and enterprise management systems. This means that a decision to accept a particular system must consider the full cost of the system over its life (which may be decades long). It cannot be just regarded as the cost of the first year's provision or initial purchase cost. Strictly evaluated tenders will always be needed for these systems, even where the provisions of the act allow a simpler procurement process.

Because of the customer loyalty built up for existing and familiar systems, a council may tend to rely on the provider of that system to an excessive extent, using them as effectively the sole supplier of hardware, software, and services for all systems. Such an arrangement should be unpackaged where possible and the various aspects put to tender; i.e. a hardware tender every three years, an operating system tender including office applications every three years, and a tender (perhaps less frequently – say every six years) for the accounting and enterprise management systems.

The IT setup comprises a number of assets which do not individually meet the capitalisation threshold but which are of substantial individual value and must therefore be tracked as "Portable and Attractive Items" or otherwise.

A person other than the IT manager needs to have an overview of the IT system, and understanding of general and council-specific IT needs and industry trends. This person should have responsibility of oversight of the IT function. This oversight could be supported by additional services from the council's internal auditor or another consultant.

It is essential to apply controls, such as enforced password changes for all systems. Many cases have been observed where, although the general system log-on is effectively password controlled, the accounting system has passwords that are unchanged from year to year; supervisor passwords are known to most staff (present and past), and standard passwords are used for guest and external positions such as auditor. This creates a substantial risk of a person who has no reason to use the accounting system having access (even supervisor access) through a system login provided for another purpose.

For example, the weighbridge operator may have a login to record weights and registrations of vehicles. If that person has access to the accounting functions, a fraud could be perpetrated by using the supervisor access to alter payroll records or invoices.

Supervisor access should be limited strictly to one or two people in the organisation who need it. Other staff should be given access only to those functions needed for their jobs. It does take some work to set up and maintain such a system but, given the risks, it is essential housekeeping. Supervisor logins should not be used except for system functions requiring them.

The IT manager or coordinator probably has supervisory access to all systems for problem solving and administration purposes. It is a very simple matter for a person in this position to make changes to records or even set up access that can be used after the individual has left the council's employment.

To reduce the risks, particular attention must be paid to tracking and verifying supervisor access. The system should require a log of all supervisory accesses. The IT manager/coordinator should also record all accesses, the reason for the access and the action taken in a diary, which is checked periodically by senior management and internal audit. These constraints apply to external IT consultants as well as to in-house staff.

When IT staff who have access to supervisory passwords leave the council, the passwords should always be changed.

16.7 Recruitment and HR

Recruitment and HR generally is an area requiring careful consideration to minimise the risks of fraud and corruption.

The Council appointment processes should be designed to avoid appointing high-risk people, particularly to positions of authority or trust.

Hiring/contracting extended family or close personal associates may raise concerns of nepotism or cronyism. In a small council area, where the pool of potential staff/contractors is small, this may be unavoidable, however all steps to ensure the person is the best candidate for the position must not only be taken but be able to stand up to scrutiny.

In addition, HR may be involved in the induction and training processes, designed to instil a respect for integrity in new and existing employees.

Appointment processes should include the following elements:

- The position is advertised widely to obtain a reasonable selection of candidates;
- The selection process is carried out in accordance with generally accepted industry standards, including wide public advertising and selection by an independent panel;
- The candidate's identity should be confirmed by photo ID and a copy retained on file;
- The candidate must supply details of at least 3 referees (including 2 employment references where the candidate has had 2 previous employments in the last 10 years);

Normally this should include the immediate previous employment.

- The candidate should state the reason for each employment terminating.
- At least 2 referees should be telephoned (including the immediate past employer). Referees should be asked specifically if the employee has ever been dishonest to the knowledge of the referee.
- The questions for the referee should be written down beforehand and the answers recorded. The referee should be asked why the candidate's employment terminated. The response needs to be checked with the reason given by the employee.
- The people taking part in the selection process must declare any conflict of interest such as having worked with the candidate previously or being related to the candidate. Generally, any person connected with any of the candidates should be excluded from the selection process.
- The selection team should produce a report showing the full result of the process for all candidates and making a reasoned recommendation. All local government employees should be appointed purely on merit.
- Special care is required where a candidate is closely connected with a senior employee. This is a situation where, intentionally or otherwise, the senior employee may influence members of the selection panel, or there may be a perception within and outside the council that a policy of "jobs for the boys" exists.
- The council should routinely obtain state and national criminal history checks for all employees before they are offered a position. If the candidate has spent a substantial time overseas, an international check should be carried out as well. It will be necessary to obtain the candidate's written consent. For senior employees and those dealing with procurement, HR, Finance, and other sensitive areas, any history of convictions, however minor and however old, should be part of

the considerations when assessing the suitability of applicants. In non-sensitive positions, only more serious or recent convictions, particularly those relating to violence, theft, or drugs will be a bar.

All employees should be required to undertake to notify the council if their personal situation changes (e.g. bankruptcy, being convicted of a criminal offence).

Employees should complete an annual declaration that they have complied with the code of conduct and fraud and corruption policies and they will do so over the next 12 months. (2).

16.8 Payroll

The largest cash expense of councils is normally payroll, making this an attractive target for fraud.

Fraudulent manipulation of payroll generally involves one of the following:

- Ghost employees with the wages paid to an account owned by the perpetrator or an associate;
- Incorrect pay rates, or allowances the employee is not entitled to;
- Manipulation of deductions;
- Incorrect timesheet entries.

Prevention measures should include:

- All payroll staff are vetted, and are fully competent to carry out their tasks;
- The payroll is regularly checked by a competent senior employee;
- All changes are notified in writing, authorised by the employee's manager, and checked and confirmed by the HR officer or CEO. This would include:

- o New employees
- o Leave arrangements
- o Deduction changes
- o One off deductions
- o Pay rate/scale changes
- o Allowance variations and special allowances
- o Advances and special pays.
- Each pay period, the audit trails for changes should be printed. The HR manager should check this against the authorisations.
- The various deduction totals should be reconciled week to week with changes where practicable;
- The clearing account should be reconciled at least monthly.
- An analysis of the payroll data may reveal discrepancies. Areas that may be worth examining are the bank accounts the pay goes to, the regularity of absences, etc.
- Routine reconciliations of payroll totals should be conducted.
- A printout of employees by department should be checked by the department managers.
- All documentation should be filed in such a way as to enable checking. Ideally one copy would be on the employee's file and a photocopy would be on a file for the pay period it related to.
- Each employee should be required to sign annually to confirm the list of deductions and allowances applied.

16.9 Debtors

A number of possibilities for fraud arise in the debtors area:

- Not invoicing for work or materials supplied, either to benefit the person to whom the items were supplied, or for an employee to obtain payment directly rather than it being made to the council;
- Not paying for items provided and then writing them off as bad debts;
- Manipulating rates and charges to provide a benefit to the perpetrator or associates;

- Taking cash received from one debtor and covering it up by allocating cash from another debtor to the first one (known as teeming and lading) and can result in snowballing deficiencies;
- Issuing duplicate or excessive invoices and then misappropriating the excess cash.

To reduce the risks in this area, a strict system of costing and invoicing work is required. The costs for all "private works" jobs should be reconciled with the invoices issued.

There should be strict control of invoice forms (as there should for all money forms). Invoices which are incorrect or otherwise cancelled should be retained in the book with the copy.

Access to the Rates and Charges database should be limited to those officers required and trusted to make changes. Audit trails of changes should be printed and checked by a senior employee.

Debtors should be asked to verify the balances on their accounts once a year, this should not be done at the year-end but done without warning at a random time.

All bad debts and other write-offs should be subject to a formal process of approval by the CEO or Council. Refunds to debtors and credit notes should be authorised by a senior employee who has checked the related documentation.

16.10 Creditors

Fraud in relation to creditors is closely linked to procurement fraud, dealt with above. However, some additional areas are:

- Ghost creditors
- Fictitious or duplicated invoices (with refund paid to the perpetrator)
- Acceptance and payment of invoices for goods or services not actually supplied.

Specific detection methods may be used to identify creditor fraud. It is also appropriate to compare vendor directorships/ownerships with current and previous employees. Current and former employees may have close links with existing employees and may use those links to perpetrate or encourage fraud or corruption.

In small and remote councils, particularly, there is the probability of close connections between staff and local businesses. This requires special vigilance to ensure fraudulent activity is likely to be detected.

Data analytics (see section 17) may identify cases for further examination.

17 Data Analytics

Data analytics is the science of examining raw data with the purpose of drawing conclusions about that information. Data analytics focuses on inference, the process of deriving a conclusion based solely on what is already known by the researcher.

Data analytics is the process of examining data to identify patterns and exceptions to those patterns. It also includes comparing data which is not normally associated to identify indications of associations.

> *An example of data analytics would be to compare the bank account numbers of employees with the bank account numbers of creditors. Any matches would require further investigation to establish if there was a legitimate reason (e.g. the employee runs a business that is the creditor).*

> *Another example would be to examine whether a group of numbers matched Benford's law. Any departure may indicate "made up" numbers.*

The above examples are not an exhaustive list of the types of data analytics which may be used.

Analysis may disclose patterns of frequency of events; again marked departures from normal patterns may show a need for further investigation.

Data analytics do not identify fraud directly. Rather, they may indicate areas where further investigation would be beneficial.

This is a specialist area, which may require the engagement of a consultant.

18 Training and induction

One of the key elements of a fraud prevention framework is creating an environment where fraud and corruption are not tolerated. To achieve this the entire workforce, councillors, and contractors must be aware of:

- What fraud and corruption are;
- Why prevention of fraud and corruption is essential for the successful operation of the council;
- How to identify indicators of fraud and corruption; and
- What to do if fraud or corruption is suspected.

Training on these aspects should be included in induction training for all relevant people before they are allowed to start work for the council. It also needs to be repeated at least every two years.

Training can be presented in many different ways, for example it may be online training, video presentations, face to face training by a live instructor or a printed course book and assessment test. There is little doubt that live instruction is the most likely to achieve a high standard of learning and to assist in generating an appropriate attitude to fraud. This form of instruction gives an opportunity to develop an understanding through an exchange between course members with different knowledge and experiences.

The training should include easily understood examples and must be followed up by individual testing.

If existing staff, councillors, and contractors have not received this training before, we recommend that a program to train all staff be conducted over a suitable period of, perhaps, two months.

Training should only be conducted by someone who has a good understanding of the subject and is able to respond to questions that may be raised. It is also essential that the trainer is committed to the council direction on fraud and corruption and is able to ensure the trainees become aligned with that direction. Training by a person who does not have this commitment can be destructive.

An outline of suitable training is included in Appendix 4 – Induction Training Module Outline

19 Maintaining the tone

Tone at the top is essential. The leadership, Mayor, Councillors, CEO, and senior managers must all be fully committed to maintaining a fraud-free, corruption-free Council. This leadership is necessary for the attitude presented to penetrate through to all Council staff.

The attitude must be demonstrated in the way the senior management behave as well as in what they say.

> *If the works manager uses a Council ute to pick up his children from school on the way home. It sends a clear message to the employees that using Council equipment for private use is acceptable.*

> *If the CEO appoints his wife as his PA, without advertising the position and getting an independent panel to conduct interviews, it is equivalent to telling the staff, "Nepotism is acceptable in this Council."*

> *If the accountant orders a new desk costing $6,000 and both raises and signs the order, it is reasonable for other staff to think that the procurement policy requiring separation of duties may be ignored.*

There is an opportunity for councils to reinforce its training and further engage employees through "lunch and learn" sessions, or similar, with presentations by outside experts as well as by senior managers. Short refresher presentations and discussion of issues could be linked with regular meetings, briefing sessions or other training.

Other opportunities for reinforcement of the tone include the induction training, refresher training, other regular and specific meetings, the council website and newsletter.

The point is that senior management will actively seek opportunities to bring fraud and corruption issues to the attention of the workforce and to give effective leadership.

20 Recording and Reporting Fraud and Corruption

Possibly the main deterrent to fraud and corruption is the knowledge that it is likely to be reported and those reports will be acted on. This requires having systems in place which make it easy for people to report suspected fraud and corruption, and which make it clear that action will be taken.

The ideal is to have a suitably senior person appointed as Integrity Officer. This allows the IO to stand apart from the council hierarchy and to present a non-confronting attitude to those reporting their concerns.

The IO need not necessarily be a staff member. An external consultant could fill this role if available. The IO needs to have a thorough understanding of the issues surrounding fraud and corruption, the way in which the various regulatory bodies work, and a basic knowledge of forensic requirements.

There must be clear guidelines for what happens when suspicions of fraud are reported. Action should be taken immediately to preserve evidence. Apart from that, particularly in the case of corruption (which must be reported immediately to the Crime and Corruption Commission), no action should be taken unless there is an immediate need, for example, to preserve Council property.

When fraud or suspected fraud is reported, the IO will take detailed notes of the allegations, the individuals involved, and any people who might be witnesses or otherwise be able to give evidence.

Anonymity can be offered to encourage employees to report their suspicions without fear of reprisals where the disclosure is under the *Public Interest Disclosure Act* (4)(PIDA). An independent IO will make it practicable for anonymous reports to be made and investigated without disclosing the informant's identity except where required by law.

The following details must be recorded:

- The person making the disclosure or the reason this is not known (e.g. anonymous disclosure under the PIDA; anonymous telephone call).
- The nature of the actual or suspected occurrence.
- A description of any asset lost, including its value or the value of any resulting or potential loss.
- The cause of the loss.
- The action taken, both to recover the loss and to prevent similar losses occurring.
- Approval for writing off the loss if it is not recovered.

In a case of corruption, there is no further investigation of the case unless the CCC directs it, either in a general direction to the CEO or in a specific direction after receiving the initial notification. Until the direction from the CCC is received, the allegation should be treated by all concerned as highly confidential and not discussed with the alleged perpetrator or anyone else.

In a case of suspected fraud of a minor nature the IO may investigate. However, if the fraud is found to be more extensive, is for a substantial amount, or if the investigation is complex, the matter should be referred to the police, and they will investigate.

It is important that Council employees do not "muddy the waters" prior to a formal investigation, by making accusations, discussing their suspicions, removing evidence, etc.

Official external reporting requirements are:

- If the fraud constitutes theft or loss of money in excess of $500 or other Council property exceeding $1,000, it must be immediately reported to the Minister and the Auditor General
- If it is a criminal offence, it must also be reported to the police.
- If it is corrupt conduct, it must also be reported to the Crime and Corruption Commission.

The IO will normally make these reports and handle all dealings with these bodies in connection with the incident, however the CEO may make the report if appropriate.

21 Resources

Councils may make use of the following publications, each of which gives a different perspective on managing the risks of fraud and corruption.

- Queensland Crime and Corruption Commission, Fraud and corruption control guidelines for best practice (CCC Guidelines)
- Queensland Audit Office – Fraud risk management – Report to Parliament 9: 2012-13(QAO Report)
- The Australian Minister for Home Affairs and Minister for Justice – Commonwealth Fraud Control Guidelines (Commonwealth Guidelines)
- Australian National Audit Office – Fraud Control in Australian Government Entities – Better Practice Guide (ANAO Better Practice Guide) and
- Standards Australia – AS 8001-2008 Fraud and Corruption Control (the Standard)

Advice on dealing with these issues is available from the Crime and Corruption Commission, and Queensland Audit Office. You may be able to get assistance from your contract auditors, other accounting firms and consultants.

The author of this book may also be able to assist you. Contact details are in the front of the book: Page iv.

Appendix 1   Council Resolution

It is Resolved That

Council considers corrupt and fraudulent conduct to be inconsistent with the activities of a local government and will not tolerate corruption or fraud on the part of the council as an entity, or on the part of the Mayor, Councillors, employees or contractors of the council, or people or entities it has dealings with.

Detailed policies and procedures are to be adopted to implement the council's view, to minimise the likelihood of fraud occurring, and to detect and deal with corrupt or fraudulent conduct if it does occur.

Appendix 2   Fraud and Corruption Framework

Clean Shire Council has a zero tolerance for fraud. In order to give effect to this and to minimise the risks of fraud and corruption this framework has been developed.

Scope and application

The framework applies to all activities of the council.

It is to be followed by all persons and firms acting for or doing business with the council including:

- The Mayor and other Councillors.
- The CEO, Directors, and managers of the council or any controlled entity.
- All employees of the council, whether full-time, part-time, permanent, or temporary.
- Volunteers performing any function for the council.
- All persons carrying out work for the council, under contract or otherwise, including all employees of contractors working on Council property or otherwise working for the council.
- All businesses entering into a contract with the council.

The framework applies from dd/mm/yyyy and continues until it is replaced or rescinded by the council.

Elements of the framework

The elements of the framework are:

- The Council resolution on Fraud and Corruption (Resolution XXXXX).

- The Fraud and Corruption Prevention Policy (Policy XXXX Adopted dd/mm/yyyy).

- The process for risk assessment for Fraud and Corruption under the policy.

- The adoption of controls to minimise the identified risks.
- Internal reporting of actual, suspected, or potential fraud and corruption.
- Recording and responding to the reported matters.
- Conducting investigations where appropriate.
- Notifying external bodies when appropriate.
- Training all employees contractors, consultants and their staff before they work for the council and at regular intervals not exceeding 2.5 years.
- Elements of the Code of conduct for employees and others.
- Annual confirmations by council workers (Appendix 6)
- Effective communication with the community.
- A fraud and corruption prevention plan with clear timelines and responsibilities.
-

Specific responsibilities

Mayor and Councillors

In their dealings with the council and their representation of the council in the community and otherwise: to conduct themselves in an ethical manner; comply with all the requirements of the Local Government Act; and to make all decisions in a fair, impartial, and unbiased manner.

Not to use their position for personal advantage for themselves or any other person or entity.

To monitor compliance with the policy and framework through consideration of the reports from the CEO, and from their contacts with the community.

Chief Executive Officer (CEO)

- Ensure the policy and framework are implemented and monitored.
- Demonstrate a high standard of personal integrity at all times and ensure all managers do the same.
- Present a report to each council meeting detailing all reports of fraud and corruption and the action taken.
- Ensure reported instances of fraud are reported to the relevant authorities and are acted on appropriately.

Managers/Directors

- Demonstrate a high standard of personal integrity at all times and ensure all supervisors and employees do the same.
- Participate in the identification of fraud risks in their areas and across the council.
- Implement controls to minimise the risks.
- Ensure all employees in their areas receive and understand the training provided.

Supervisors

- Demonstrate a high standard of personal integrity at all times and ensure staff do the same.
- Ensure suspected or actual fraud or corruption is reported to the Integrity Officer

Integrity officer

- Manage the fraud and corruption control process throughout the council
- Develop, implement, and maintain the policy,
- Conduct induction and refresher training,
- Facilitate the risk assessment by managers and others,
- Receive reports of suspected, actual or potential fraud and corruption
- Notify authorities as appropriate,
- Ensuring the appropriate records are kept,

- Advise the CEO on action to be taken, and
- Advise employees and others who may have potential ethical issues such as conflict of interest.

All council workers

- Maintain a high standard of personal integrity.
- Not be involved in, support, or ignore fraud or corruption.
- Report any suspicions of fraud or corruption to the integrity officer.
- Not discuss their suspicions with others.

Appendix 3   Fraud and Corruption Implementation Plan

This plan will require substantial modification to allow for local conditions ant position titles in each council. In particular, some of the steps may have been completed and the order of steps may need to be modified. Specific timing will depend on the requirements of the council but we recommend that councils should complete most of the process within 6 months of commencement and put the whole structure in place within one year.

Action	Responsibility	Complete by	Done
Initial presentation to councillors and commitment by Council	CEO		
Prepare/Adopt initial Fraud and Corruption Policy	CSM/Council		
Appoint Integrity Officer(IO)	CEO		
Conduct information session for managers	IO/CEO		
Prepare framework	IO		
Perform risk assessments	EMT(IO)		
Prepare risk register	IO		
Identify treatments/controls for risks	Managers/(IO)		
Review policy and framework	IO/CEO		
Identify and implement changes to policies, code of conduct, etc	IO/Managers		
Develop training modules	IO		
Develop explanatory packages for employees, contractors, councillors, businesses, the community,	IO		

including web pages, handouts, information sessions			
Letter from CEO to employees, contractors, businesses	IO/CEO		
Put reporting structures in place (Internal and external)	IO		
Conduct training of employees, contractors, consultants	IO		
Conduct training for councillors	IO/CEO		
Community information sessions for businesses and the community	IO/CEO		
Develop ongoing plans and procedures	IO		

Abbreviations:

CEO – Chief Executive Officer

EMT – Executive Management Team

IO – Integrity Officer

CSM – Corporate Services Officer

( ) indicates Facilitated By

Appendix 4 Induction Training Module Outline

Introduction
Introduce everyone
Discharge preconceptions – put issues on whiteboard
Explain agenda

What are fraud and corruption?
Include examples. Show how starting from the lowest level and working up can result in understating the severity of examples. Discuss minimum levels requiring action.

Include examples from many areas

- Decisions not made impartially,
- Nepotism and cronyism,
- Procurement fraud
- False tendering (connected tenderers)
- Bribery
- Corrupt behaviour by the council
- Supplier offering a benefit

Why is fraud important?
The risk and cost to local government
The impact on Council finances, jobs, and services provided
Impact on trust
Integrity requirements in legislation
Consequences for the individual

What is Council's stance?
Zero tolerance
Fraud and Corruption Policy

Who commits fraud?

Councillors, employees, consultants, contractors, suppliers – everyone.

How to identify fraud

Red flags – Transactional and behavioural

What should you do about fraud?

Look out for it

Prevent it

Report it

- When, How, and to Whom

Don't commit it or turn a blind eye

What happens next?

Who is it reported to?

How is it investigated?

What action is taken?

- Reporting
- Recovery
- Dealing with the perpetrator
- Preventing future occurrences

Test understanding

Suggested individual written test

Summary of Key learning points

Appendix 5   Training Schedule/Record

Last Name	First name	2016	2017	2018	2019	2020
Smith	Arthur	20/1/16	30/11/17		15/11/19	
Jones	Henry	20/1/16	30/11/17		15/11/19	
Absolom	Albert	31/3/16	30/11/17		Left	
Johnson	Mary		18/6/17		15/5/19	

Appendix 6   Personal declaration

To Clean Shire Council

I confirm that:

1) I have received and understood the following
    a) Fraud and Corruption Policy
    b) Code of Conduct
2) I have received training in my obligations in respect of fraud and corruption
3) I understand that I must not become involved or support fraud or corruption in relation to the council
4) I understand my duty to report any suspicions of fraud or corruption in accordance with the policy
5) I confirm that since (a) the commencement of my engagement with the council/(b) the last confirmation [delete one]
    a) I have not been involved in any fraudulent or corrupt conduct.
    b) I have complied with the council policies and code of conduct and will do so in the future
    c) I have not been charged with any criminal offence, made bankrupt, or entered into an arrangement with my creditors

Name	
Position	
Relation to Council	Councillor/Employee/Consultant/Contractor/Supplier/ Volunteer [Delete as appropriate]
Signature	
Date	

Appendix 7   Fraud and Corruption Policy

Clean Shire Council

Date Adopted:	x/xx/yyyy
Review date:	x/xx/yyyy
Council Resolution No.	x-xxx/yyyy

1.   Background

Council recognises that fraud and corruption are major risks, which can adversely affect the ability of the council to achieve its objectives.

This policy is intended to minimise the risk of Fraud or corruption occurring in the council or affecting the council.

2.   Definitions

- **Fraud** is obtaining a personal advantage through deception
- **Corruption** is using a position of power or trust to obtain a personal advantage
- **Personal advantage** includes advantage for family, friends, associates, or an entity connected to a person. It also includes an unwarranted disadvantage to another person.
- A **position of trust** includes any public office, employment, appointment, or contract.
- Theft from an employer is taken to be **fraud**.
- **Corrupt behaviour** may be by an entity other than a person.
- **Corrupt behaviour** includes enabling or permitting another to engage in corrupt behaviour.

The full definitions in the *Australian Standard AS 8001-2008* and the *Crime and Corruption Act 2001* are included in the appendix.

- **Council Worker** includes a Councillor, an employee of the council or a controlled entity whether full time, part time, or temporary, a volunteer, a contract worker or a consultant carrying out work for the council.

- Council means Clean Shire Council

3. Legislation and Sources

Australian Standard AS 8001-2008
Crime and Corruption Act 2001 (Qld)
Public Interest Disclosure Act 2010 (Qld)
Local Government Act 2009(Qld)
Criminal Code Act 1899 (Qld)
Public Sector Ethics Act 1994 (Qld)

4. Policy

4.1. Zero Tolerance

Council has a zero tolerance for fraud and corruption. This means that the council will not employ, or engage in business relationships with anyone who commits an act of fraud or corrupt behaviour on, on behalf of, or in connection with the council.

Employees who are found to have been involved in, knowingly allowed, or supported such acts will be dismissed.

Others who have a business relationship with the council and commit such an act will have their relationship with the council terminated and will be liable to compensate the council for any loss resulting from the act or the termination of the arrangement.

4.2. Preventative measures

The Chief Executive Officer (CEO) must:

1. Ensure that a full analysis of fraud and corruption risks is carried out within 3 months of first adoption of this policy and every two years thereafter.

2. Prepare and implement a Fraud and Corruption Risk Management Plan.

3. Ensure all policies including those relating to procurement and appointment and promotion of employees have appropriate measures to minimise the risks of fraud and corruption.

4. Ensure the procedures including those relating to procurement, appointment and promotion of employees, and making any decision are adequate to minimise the risks of fraud and corruption.

5. Ensure the code of conduct for Council workers is adequate to minimise the risks of fraud and corruption.

6. Put in place procedures for reporting fraud or corrupt behaviour to an appropriate officer; whether they have occurred or are likely to occur, are known or are suspicions.

7. Appoint a suitably experienced person (employee or consultant) as Integrity officer to
    a. receive reports,
    b. make appropriate records,
    c. report the incidents to appropriate authorities (Crime and Corruption Commission; Department of Infrastructure, Local Government and Planning; Queensland Audit Office; and the Police Service),
    d. carry out investigations where appropriate,
    e. make recommendations to the CEO for appropriate action in respect of the incident to address the particular incident and to reduce the risk of a similar incident occurring, and
    f. To advise employees and others on issues related to ethical behaviour.

8. Ensure initial and regular training is carried out to ensure all employees, councillors and other Council workers are familiar with their duties in relation to fraud and corruption and are

aware of the need to take a proactive approach to fraud prevention.

All **Council Workers** including councillors, contractors, and consultants must:

1. Act with integrity and in an ethical manner in all dealings connected with the council.
2. Comply with the applicable code of conduct, policies, and procedures determined by the council or CEO.
3. Be proactive in detecting, preventing, and reporting fraud and corruption in accordance with the code of conduct and policies

4.3. *Reporting*

1. All suspected or identified instances of fraud or corruption must be reported immediately to the Integrity officer except:
   a. If they involve the integrity officer – in which case they should be reported to the CEO;
   b. The integrity officer cannot be contacted – in which case they should be reported to the CEO
   c. They relate to a councillor other than the mayor and the person reporting them is a councillor or the CEO – in which case they should be reported to the CEO or the Mayor
2. To enable the investigator to obtain evidence admissible in a court, suspected fraud or corruption should not be investigated, or discussed with <u>anyone</u> other than the person to whom it is reported, until it has been reported and a direction to investigate has been given by the Integrity officer or the CEO.
3. Corruption must not be investigated until the CCC has been notified and has given an instruction to investigate it.
4. Criminal activity must not be investigated unless authorised by the police.

5. No incident must be discussed with the suspected perpetrator without authority.
6. Subject to any legal constraints, the CEO must report to Council all instances of fraud or corruption and the action taken.

4.4. *Recovery*

Council will take reasonable efforts to recover any loss arising through fraud or corruption. However, before incurring substantial costs in legal action, the council will take advice on the likely cost and the chances of recovery of the loss.

5. Review of policy

This policy will be reviewed in the event of changes to any of the underlying legislation or at the expiry of two years from the date of adoption.

6. Appendix to policy – Definitions of fraud and corruption

| Fraud | Fraud is defined in the Australian Standard AS 8001-2008 as: Dishonest activity causing actual or potential financial loss to any person or entity including theft of moneys or other property by employees or persons external to the entity and where deception is used at that time, immediately before or immediately following the activity. This also includes the deliberate falsification, concealment, destruction or use of falsified documentation used or intended for use for a normal business purpose or the | |

	improper use of information or position for personal financial benefit	
	The theft of property belonging to an entity by a person or persons internal to the entity but where deception is not used is also considered 'fraud' for the purposes of the Standards.	
Corruption	Corrupt conduct is defined under the Crime and Corruption Act 2001 (Qld) s.15 as:	
	conduct of a person, regardless of whether the person holds or held an appointment, that—	
	• adversely affects, or could adversely affect, directly or indirectly, the performance of functions or the exercise of powers of—	
	- a unit of public administration (UPA)	
	or	
	- an individual person holding an appointment in a UPA	
	• results, or could result, directly or indirectly, in the performance of functions or the exercise of powers mentioned above in a way that—	
	- is not honest or is not impartial	
	- involves a breach of the trust placed in a person holding an appointment,	

		either knowingly or recklessly	
		- involves a misuse of information or material acquired in or in connection with the performance of functions or the exercise of powers of a person holding an appointment	
		• is engaged in for the purpose of providing a benefit to the person or another person or causing a detriment to another person	
		• would, if proved, be—	
		- a criminal offence	
		or	
		- a disciplinary breach providing reasonable grounds for terminating the person's services, if the person is or were a holder of an appointment.	

Appendix 8   CEO letter

CLEAN SHIRE COUNCIL

Date:_____

From: Chief Executive Officer

To: The Mayor, and Councillors, all employees and contract employees of the council, all consultants, and advisors, all businesses with whom the council has dealings.

FRAUD AND CORRUPTION

This letter summarises the council's position on fraud and corruption. Broad definitions are:

Fraud is the obtaining of a personal advantage for yourself or someone else by deception.

Corruption is using of your appointment or position to obtain an advantage for yourself or another.

Fraud includes bribery, which is making undisclosed payments to people to influence their actions.

Fraud also includes theft or unauthorised personal use of Council property by employees.

Council has zero tolerance of fraud and corruption.

Fraud could be on the part of an employee, or someone dealing with the council. Council will take action in every case of discovered fraud or corruption. For employees, this will normally result in dismissal.

All employees are required to report immediately any known or suspected incidence of Fraud or Corruption to the Integrity officer (John Smith). Employees should not investigate the incident unless authorised to do so by John Smith or myself. John will decide what action needs to be taken, will record the details of the incident, and notify myself and any authority (Police, Crime and Corruption Commission, or the Department) as required.

John will accept anonymous reports where the legislation allows this, but it is preferable to disclose the name of the person making the report, as further information may be needed for the investigation of the complaint, also it ensures you will not, subsequently, be considered to have failed to report something you knew about.

In any investigation, discretion will be observed to prevent recrimination against the person reporting. The *Public Interest Disclosure Act* (4) provides protection against recrimination where it applies.

The Council is putting in place a number of measures to minimise the likelihood of fraud and corruption, and to detect it if it does occur.

Training will be carried out to help you recognise and prevent fraud and corruption. This training is compulsory for all employees, contract employees and consultants. The training will also be incorporated into existing induction training for new staff.

I would ask you to remain vigilant and assist the council in preventing and identifying any unethical conduct.

I.M.A. CEO

Chief Executive Officer.

22 Bibliography

1. **Queensland Audit Office.** *Fraud Management in Local Government.* Brisbane : Queensland Audit Office, 2015. ISSN 1834-1128.

2. **Standards Australia.** *AS 8001-2008 Fraud and Corruption Control.* Sydney : Standards Australia, 2008.

3. **Queensland Government.** Crime and Corruption Act 2001. 2001.

4. —. Public Interest Disclosure Act 2010. *Public Interest Disclosure Act 2010.* 2010.

5. **Australian National Audit Office.** *Public Sector Governance - Volume 1.* Canberra : Australian National Audit Office, 2003.

6. **Chartered Accountants Australia and New Zealand.** *Are Australia and New Zealand Corrupt?* Melbourne : Chartered Accountants Australia and New Zealand, 2015.

www.ingramcontent.com/pod-product-compliance
Lightning Source LLC
Chambersburg PA
CBHW071440210326

41597CB00020B/3888